microaggressions

Erik Stinson is an American writer and creative director working in New York City. His interests include shopping, fashion and ancient history.

microaggressions
erik stinson

Thanks to Jess, Will, Sam and Sophie. Thanks to Blake and Gene. Thanks to Weston, Ingrid and Dallas. Thanks to my family, friends (in Seattle, Oakland, New York, elsewhere) and co-workers. Thanks to Jackie and my cats. Special thanks to my dad for the quiet and the scotch.

global look and feel   11

desk pains   37

shopping sweat   53

augmented reality   69

contract talks   95

going private   105

global look and feel

witches

firmly hold the cooing
goat god of cheap
christmas lights
construction workers
freebase dirty speed

satellite phone

the markets die
extreme volatility
a difficult phone call
on the roof of that
japanese hotel

mass display

eye-catching shelf wobbler
laminated case stacker
end cap for the ages
holiday custom
price card

1980s cop show

two fast boats flying
down a canal in miami
here's the subtext
wet dim afternoon
whitecaps

the teen tv years

sneaking out at night
to visit boyfriend
at the hospital

institutional barriers

wet cola bottle in my television
steak with her congressmen
the judge cool medicated
in her small blue convertible
dreaming of lavish endowments
then smoking parliaments
in the situation room

necrophilia

common fairlane
ambien surf club
orb gazpacho
killing palms

speaking in turns

for women there's danger
in being ahead of trend
like the fear of too red lips
or telling a joke that makes
the wrong person laugh

compelling

the bulk of earth's wealth
pushed like so much cheese
through hundreds of miles
of PowerPoint presentations
being stolen and bought
for all those dead eyes

wisdom in summer

the air in san francisco
is sweet orange juice soda
blood on ruby on rails
palo alto vista
i try to sell my tears
to children born inside
the softest machine
1995–2001

bill blass

deadstock corderoy
supple campomaggi
leather bag nwt
you can understand
by touching
material

tv

i like older shows
forgotten plot arcs
seasoned stage actors
the cobwebs of
bygone regimes

wife

her perfect-ten sigh
seated right in
the Range Rover
as we return from
dropping off
some hot guns

domination

The Gap proves
an excellent retail model
even when we're slightly too close
to the food court

the classic rock format

uncle's Camaro
wet fields behind
the baseball diamond
goin' in on white girl
before high school reunion

2020

liz warren interviewed on wnyc
cannabis sativa
equal pay for
all our divas

distinctive fins

longline swimwear
sun sand soon
the tiberium
collection on
purple disc

sleep technology

wearing heavy armour
go unconscious on a downtown train
i want to be ready for death
on an unplanned jog
people see my black slick of
next season's Gore-Tex outerwear

Subaru hatchback

ten amazing years
in exile from my
rusting province
twin peaks on vhs
smoke salmon
gift set

growth

massive german telecom group
has shady business with
volume in prime wood commodities
the long day's abstracted mood
on three Bloomberg terminals
at his downbeat Water Street paradise

mobile site

you imagine open
desert then a small
patch of white cloth
look closer at extensive tenting
de-selected mosquitoes

jennifer performance solutions

high hopes about a
new position in
creative development
until the corporate site
opens another slash job
three quarters negative and
inexcusable stock photography

desk pains

stock picks

you think of traders in corner
offices or you think of municipal
golf course guys
cheap cigars
deals on hot tubs

fashion mistake

mesh on lace
a creamy wool
the hat who still
doesn't speak
business thai

lana remix

i'm doing the central valley
in a borrowed Accura
the Accord-sized one
in black with gold trim
it's 4 a.m. and i'm actually
ready to die for the feeling

men

it rained   inside
men of the marina bar
saying loud things like
her body was dangerous
those projects might have
been the end of his career
we're under water
on the summer house

third jazz age

can you imagine an
upright bass among premium
furnishings marble sink with
open bluetooth display
archival stork club designs
for the salon area and
a barely-tech worker
off the job getting faded on
fermented dessert fruit
welling up from clay jars
filthy sustaining arcology

sage

poison on
a stone table
heavy worn curtain
a fine suit of
clubwear

productiv

on the screen
a candelabra
fragments of a reply
intimate files
turkish zippers
made from brass

occult

biopower could be
about geometry or
sex or just really
well-made
leather bags

forgotten snake brand

hell yeah i was
on ski bus that hard winter
we would even skateboard
in a parking garage when
it got heavy outside and i did
Lee Pipes with wet hems
cold socks with holes

scammer

call now and belong
worried young woman
seat yourself upon
the lip of success

drug cave

i explained collective bargaining
with a fast digital painting
torn wool and the winter sun
a meeting of sweat
and confirmed indifference

tattoo content

academics and art critics
tend to write against skin
rarely on the body
but that's my hotspot for cool
all these inside jokes about
boring people in good shoes

job creator

call the big plug of the metro spice corridor
empty duplex skinny designer television
topless sorters part-time overseer in
    a track suit
this door muscle guy fully auto brick
    of choiceless steel
before the sexy interface club delivery
    business all
evergreen chambers and low clouds on
    the freeway

shopping sweat

air crisis

dave feel good
on his skateboard
in the halfpipe
everything free
tiffany speak
language
of men
gaining speed
dave leaves
the bowl
forever

faith and Absolut Vodka

years before i starved
the business it was
normal to spend three
loaded trucks on a
sacrifice to the youth
a ten-month media
plan was luxe cathedral
the body the blood the
street team kissing
my whitelabel crombie
before i leave for
executive dinner tribeca

nude saints

everything encourages
her to die well-worn like
St John's Bay outerwear
party Gecko Hawaii
go Raven SDL small
hugs in Big Dogs 4XL
exploit JNCO
No Fear

williamsburg traditional

the ancient digital library
computer subroutine where
a few old files rest   walk
or   play cards half-watching
star trek alone

qumran

after history
the waters from those cliffs
emerging spiritually pure
in the modern granite kitchen
above the ending desert city
to write of the bending
internal plague and
a service economy
total war

after silk

color catalog array
against the back wall
with almost amphibian
design cues on white tile
Raf Simons seams
when i retrieve
the violence of
that retired design
just for you from
the Prada mainframe
we acquired at auction

snow falling on cedars

the poisonwood bible
bridges of madison county
captain corelli's mandolin

oakland california

i regret anything
the sun and moon
cold drinks at the cemetery
so white the starlight
powder and myself
as a leonid image

bassline

in the shadow of the
beach hotel i waited
to watch a pool of time
in the sun of the far east
the black suv crept along
oceanfront avenue

publicity

two people
walking upstream in
fashionable malibu
french-designed but
italian-made fabrics
suddenly paparazzi from a side street
the movement of glass eyes in ecstasy
women everywhere pressing on them
like the finest egyptian cotton

sunglass

divorced single dad carries
la beretta for his job in
primetime network television
goes to the gym alone
wears sweaters as shirts

drawl

comfortable career
winds ebbing you
find yourself looking
for another new city
with late summer gardens
raleigh baton rouge
greenville sc

augmented reality

purple tuesday

mirrored lenses
at the remembered club
the jazz isn't about you
another hard downturn
puts me on my ass
under the e-cigarette glow
at the back of the latest
groovy bread line

citadel

a blurred bank logo
on the deserted common park
at the global center of ideas
nobody can afford
to walk the distance between dreams
browse any takeout app for information
access the latest new color
arrive silently with
troops from the west
at the gate of the city
to pay whatever the
market feels

red light

in the haunted streets
of summer on the edge of fire
a perfect union of sequence
a date becoming a history
the woman on camera
seeing herself in the dusk
a thousand years of Other

intertext

young kids in bands
decide to stop naming
art projects after their
magazine obsessions
i'm bummed about that
the state of teen punk art
i have bad dreams in winter
of ghosts wearing fast fashion
revealing their night powers
at the secret club
like so many waylaid brand directors
the ripping jive opiates his
torn literary ego as if
we should all buy

dominion

a low part of old town
where the plants have thoughts
and four imported car dealerships
share the same failing gas station

new plague

blessed by amazing supervision
thinking back to fast emails
re-living an excellent debrief
i consider myself high on this process
of refined destruction and
our emotional economic decline

spectacular

scanned paperback thriller
exposed male nipples
guy debord finally free from pain
the paper & coffee before
profit and peer review
her personalized nameplate
access discount code
on daily inspiration her
maximum visibility lifestyle prison

liberation theology

speaking to god's boss
on my way to Kia mecca
to score real park avenue junk
with internet brand analytics
buy a few cheap data scientists
for my impure mango mega hedge
running the street squeeze
in a steady credit rain
caught under the awning as ever
another splashy price bubble
seen by very few blue chips

the richly hosted cache people
of this hidden corporate tapestry
an Avalon Hybrid in AutoCAD
watching the da vinci machine

on public YouTube de-synched
audio before bed
another brutal ISIS birth video
as like the perfect business model

froyo baroness

control without obligation
convenience as a kind of war
against history and the self
for this coming spring season
we are seeking a profound change in
consumer behavior

combat tourism

seventy dollar
armored water supply
strapped and sleepy
in the bed of this huge
white Toyota Tundra
the desert passing
life standing still
for her

death project

brick and high ceilings
the super-wanted residue of industry
pottery by several creative directors
excellent large sinks and
discreet access to the ocean

screen con

whole days like this
supervising a sort of black site
product developer retained and
waiting in our rented volcano lair
seven computers in a circle
teen macaroni box asset folder
rare archival-quality lizard jpeg
on reflective package coating
the renewed aggravation of the feeds
when we quote a price on scope
image research budget exhausted

merchandising politics

drug business after kentucky
spatula tortellini Ferrari tour
four-night outdoor screening
against red rocks with
mostly members of The Eagles
their CD album of cocaine b-sides
playing the stalled cinnamon mirage

microaggressions

after the detroit gig
i bought a 98 Cadillac
from one of those
white people car apps
nothing mattered
in the bitch seat
art was possible for me

office classic

dusky blood brow
strata cumulous in the
western landscape painting
behind her Onkyo or the
discrete cubano folding
tray of wet onyx
and this gold-look
scientific calculator all
cinema quality

quarantine

gaudy paralegal prints
ambition commitment teamwork
three button suit
nile waters LLC
lately-erected four-star hotel
on basically my desert
cartoon warning label
unshared secrets of the
direct mail business

tech deck

1990s skateboarding brands
were ahead of the times
clothed in the dead youth culture
and manufactured in china
in the multinational style
our toxic earnings statements
our centralized shipping costs

certified neutrals

i want the one
that makes me feel
like ancient money
with young children
Eileen Fisher cloaks
shaded soy candle
reconsidered terrarium
$600 etchings of
exhumed tee shirts
from the 95 winter
collection

military-inspired look

dull violet light
from the bare tube above
an open wardrobe
i spent years trying
to express this
non-feeling of
a man wearing
clothes

virtual retail

when you fail at hellish things
i airlift the crocodile tote
bottled water is immediate
plus your beige linen thing
goes on some corporate tab

full seduction

a secret blue from here to
this beachy area with more of like
that stumbling shoegaze look
the darker teens of central europe
grown and fully employed
in bronze skin all along
invisible italy

le tempo rouge

weird how every grid
has the gold coast topography
the trick is to go in
a few years before the slide
find your future power broker
seated at the lowest bar level
le tempo rouge off central avenue
bushwick new york u.s.a. earth
becoming a scotch glass
aligned with my prosumer glide

contract talks

delicate piping

i'm getting into jazz again
guilty music and fucked and
i don't belong anywhere now
but but but that's the power
these big culture bullies can't
simulate good sex with their
hip winter clothing for
white women to crave
in the grand scheme
of the group chat

2007

baby project of the
well-to-do dressers
and famous friends
never really growing
on to their own
brilliant tableau
hollywood parties
1992 the last new
celebrities of the
data productivity era
still banging around
on the scene like 67

ova pariah

writing again
for my spanish television beat
in the dark back garden
her summer goals collage beside me
his boyfriend's
car magazine in the
headless brooklyn
afternoon

commodity chic

perhaps a bad time to think
of the spokane indian reservation
though with route 66 at the back
of my mind who knows ?
we lost the Cadillac pitch twice
and now for this new nameplate of
japanese pickup truck well i tell ya
when i'm leading the sell
everything sort of becomes my process

i say   *remember the back of the cereal box ?*
as i explain our optics to the lead client

i say   *consider the lava lamp's digitality*
i remind her that back-end development
isn't my concern

i say   *you didn't bring me here to
think about costs*

i freeze and re-invent eye contact
i say   *the choice you have to make
is between three distinct dreams*

die for the feeling

when you find love
and someplace in the sun
the horrors of night still
follow you at a distance
like adam levine
wearing Valentino
in the life-insurance
commercial about
everything

canali desert club

the author
jon leon remains
alive after xanadu
printed information 1998
every cruel business
the tristate clouds

going private

hampton jitney

the estate was cold
as she arrived
on a thursday afternoon
to clean the tennis courts
during a light rain
the sportcoat in ruin
rumpled red cashmere blouse
several dull knives wiped
clean on scottish grass

lucky iguana LLC

we're speaking spanish
with a chinese accent
in The Sky private casino
downtown brooklyn snow falling
trying to throw the world series
of Nissan street racing unlimited

teen witch

when we
reinvented drag
that was the winter
in the dog tooth lofts
candles burning fast
waxed black jackets
the recession settling over
secondary markets like
 blistering chemical fog

millennial freedom

a political assassination
inside the soho boutique
he went into the hard gallery light
the eternal shopping music played
a tribute to real desire

everlong

i see a river
like in a video game
scenes with no edges
very little open sky
mythic sports cars
pure white sneakers

microaggressions
Erik Stinson

Published by Test Centre in 2016
in an edition of 300 copies

Text copyright © Erik Stinson

Design: Thom Swann for A New Archive

Cover art: Zane Lewis, *UNTITLED (SPEED)*,
2015, lacquer on canvas, 224 × 163 cm
Reproduced courtesy of the artist

Printed by ArtQuarters Press

ISBN: 978-0-9935693-0-2

testcentre.org.uk